JOURNAL

PETER PAUPER PRESS, INC.
WHITE PLAINS, NEW YORK

Cover image by Ann Johnstone for Jane Mosse Designs

Copyright © 2008
Peter Pauper Press, Inc.
202 Mamaroneck Avenue
White Plains, NY 10601
All rights reserved
ISBN 978-1-59359-479-4
Printed in China
7 6 5 4 3 2 1

Visit us at www.peterpauper.com

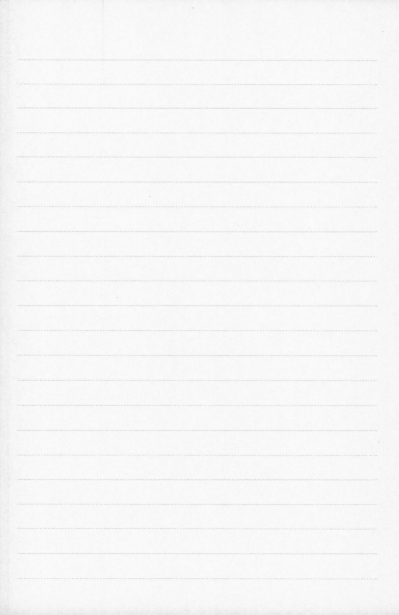